Open
Epic

Cover art by Norma Cole.

First Edition, 2017
ISBN 978-0-692-82724-6 (Paperback)
Library of Congress Control Number: 2017942181

Acknowledgments:

A version of "Hilda's Hunting" was first published in 2008 as a chapbook
by *Macaw Macaw Press* through the Dusie Kollectiv (Bonnie Jean Michalski).
"Open Epic" appeared in *Aufgabe*, Issue 12 under a different title (Erin
Morrill & Jamie Townsend). "Plural Bell" was published as an *LRL
Textile Series* chapbook in 2012 (Dawn Pendergast). The author wishes to
elaborately & sincerely thank the editors of these publications.

For the people whose conversation & advice aided in the composition of
these poems, the author wishes to thank them in person or by mail.

For their wonderful books, for their choosing of this one, the author wishes
to thank Brad Vogler, Crane Giamo, & Jared Schickling.

For their time & attention, the author is in the deep swell of debt &
gratitude to Norma Cole, Susan Gevirtz, & Tyrone Williams.

Delete Press
Fort Collins, CO
Lockport, NY
Salt Lake City, UT
deletepress.org

Open
Epic

Julia Drescher

For C –
You are good to me.

[through her]

Hilda's Hunting

11

Open Epic

43

Hands Chalk the Walls

55

Plural Bell

71

through her

the emptying

forms

loans, love, loam,
long, long –

long gone

Hilda's
Hunting

Hunting is about
Completing the sentence

Our sweet HILDA has begun
"Our sweet HILDA"

Perhaps remakes where we

Where a stranger waits

Begins at as will you

Come back the last time I saw you

Was a drier dusk already again

DEEP IN what sentenced the woods

Stark light slices

Nicely scores in

Trees what made for

Tracks transparent

Bodies made seen

& for shining fall in

Line head first

Where something was

Crueler festers where

Our HILDA has seen the sweet men go out

to hunt by day she

stands transfixed by knots her eyes

grasp our HILDA had your eyes

an assumption an attempt

                                        The men go out

to establish a code

Regrow attire

Hunting is about
The hunt meaning
Something & such
Force one more than one
Containing such as
More than one such
& such waiting on beasts
& are our means for
Hunting hares using
Hounds are for coursing
Out & horses & hunters
With knives &/or guns
For both gentle & dangerous
Ones such as
For deer for boar for bears in
Woods are still common
Enough wolves too could
Make the hunt
Last for several

Does not know our HILDA

how or what

A gun

Perhaps HILDA

    each night

Collects heads
For her own neck
Pretends her shoulders
As wide as the measured
Land as thick

HILDA is at once

sad &

not-sad

she holds
like these
her hands
she holds
these like
her hands
hold
like is to
pretend as

& in her hand some shine & in her hand some bruise

Each night walks HILDA down in

The woods are a treatise

A sentence is

About each
Starting out
Repeats another
& another

"The hunter shall..."

Techniques in the making
Unharbour ways out from to
Home out of (dark) woods
Moist & warm

HILDA is game for

The book of hunting divides

Animals twice into gentle

Beasts & savage beasts was

The animal common

Or not enough

Long sticks to hold the line

Pressed on as if

What was leaking

Followed what was

Next shoulders

Clicks & rattles split

& how to cover it up

"Our sweet HILDA sometimes runs amok."

Startle out

Or else was

Waits for little

Else in a given location HILDA

Seizes upon sees

Built up false

Fences for traps for what

Could be done with

& wants to

Close in the woods what else would run

At NIGHT hunts how?

Is about clawing the sentence out

Was once the animal has been gutted

The carcass turned

Over & made to stand

We were more

sad than not

more meat

Our

Sweet

Sometimes

Our HILDA
WANTS

Who's sure

What order

The body goes

Should never be changed

HILDA knows we see

Her accordingly she

Refuses merely to re

–fuse such rules such

Acts out she

Leads with feet with hands

& the belly of

This beast all sounds

Where our
Sweet HILDA
has surely
begun you
have her
eyes if I
see you
again I'll
be able to

As slee the hert with strengthe not

Traps pits enclosures the

Book of hunting explains certain

Signs say exhaustion as in

Then the game had run its courses

Begun mouth open & toes

Spread & both now tightly closed

Taking to water the hunt

Plunged that is to say after it

As all a means of teaching our

HILDA

HILDA

The hunter shall be reticent about

Surprise techniques what

Commonly

Enough we have seen

The sweet men go out enough

A slip knot spring mechanism hangs

wolf upside   down

& tearing still growling could

lick its own familiar pathway

out laid below its tracks   still

Bread is added to the
blood daytime mean-
while locked in her room
HILDA would dream
of boars it seems
right their bodies
her body leans to for
rest her fingers their grinders
hurt beneath the door
let us in let us
pretend sweet HILDA
from under the door diminutive shadows diminutive snores

When not once our HILDA
calls out her wants all wants
for her mouth wants steel
                    jaws

shame gnaws all through
the same she goes
for days eating nothing
says as sweetly she
is saving herself for
                    God

Covered thicket older corbin bones
still rigid whites hanging just
As heavy from
Limbs just as

                                        Whatever else there was THERE
                                        Was our sweet sweet HILDA
                                        Sometimes we know

                                        She'd tell

Some beasts we know still breathe

MEANWHILE
On roughly

Hewn trails HILDA
Finds Huntsman

Droppings

                    Showing them to the moon

Were also in
danger then

The hunt must
Keep its

Distance must
In such larger danger

Whisper

The sentence

could not be

more open

intention is

the gun is

pleasure in

SUCH FEARS HILDA hides there

Is such a cleaner cure

Like curing like go on

Pretend what wants you still I

HILDA sweet HILDA we will

Say please

Fall in

Line up

Gummed

Parts next

                              We don't
                              We don't
                              We don't we
                              Never

                                   Do not

                              Ever at

No – yours

First say please

Pretend it

A game

Hunting is about the rules
Were cord axes scissors
For binding cutting binding what cut
Grindstone flints there
Were similar tools calls
For the pack *hole hole hole* or
A single long note perhaps a

Giving up   dragging
Along the ground pieces of meat
Circle the blood to draw the wolf
In complete its round &
Shut it up thus   We can not stop
                                             Else
                                             Where we scatter

Meaning such as moaning means

Fills creekly as water would our hearts were dry

& hiding

                                                            We said somewhere
                                                            Out loud *Please*
                                                            Put. It. Down.

As such

Places in

Place of bereavement

O God HILDA we swear we wanted
to tell you sweet HILDA there was
a time when there was
no horse we didn't love no
question but that whether
to want is to waste

All then

Pull in
Tight &
Tighter
See
Still we
Do love

As can be seen by mouths first gaping then gnashing into the ground

No tougher meat

Our HILDA perhaps

Our hiding heart bone begun warming

What rights of warren

Still thrilling what chase what viscera

Delicious our sad to say reports our

Foot festers brutal our aches all hour

Clicks or rattles that is to say

Whatever else   we had our

Hearts battered

No better HILDA

Open
Epic

"You're tired,"
one of them said, "You don't want
to build the city."

"Yes, I'm tired,"
I said & sat down on a boulder
near the spring

Bleeding freely

& sold or kept or sold & kept or sold

Our names are our name

Scatherings, leaking sores

     Glutter &

        ,more dim,

          Glow

On flat land

Black branches blue sky

& a man his daughter

In his hands her severed hands

Left the light —still

The light left kept

Sun-scour, cicada sift

mesquite

& so sad his see
up there there is
no crown on thm

& weeping we gone
slouching evry cleft
"we gone down

& unable to "die
down in it

twigs in boltered hair
aslant shoulders her

a constitution shreds

and her all and

and her every trouble slow
murmur then unheard of

ferocity | hand-made

organs dark fists

God's own goddamn

soul

the gutter

horse
or she

from the root

    "kurs" –

        hors
        hars
        hers

    "to run"

from horse to

        hoarse
        hearse
        hearsay

keep *from*
collapsing

    "a stay apparatus"

& sold or kept or sold & kept or sold

Someone Found
Not a lady no more

As in,
The "Etc. Etc."
Of <u>Texas</u>

Hands
Chalk
The Walls

for M – & M –

smear

    drops its canary

        to leave   shapes

              as downward

                  shows

its green

through

with you

    ...

a ghost *behind*

its middling its

run   once

seen see it

behind every

one

    ...

so close to child   is *not*

                                                            the same as

                                                            is

                                    drawn
                        ships

                        ...

but if the blue's

not water

haul

        cave to *hull*

                        negotiate the face as

                smudged   the eye

                                        still

                                        clear

of *slips*

                        ...

57

wailing across

waves hiss

hard hits

the stomach

all salt

   ...

a jar

 every

  thing found

   in

    mouths

     gently

     as taken

     out

   ...

slight pelvis-like drip –

a scarab

without

its iridescence

        ...

  horses

     legs *and* air

        bloating   trip

            over and over

               (it)

      ...

            pry pretty from

            meaning (something

                 plastic)

      ...

runs magenta without its light in as much as

sound its walking as petal after petal effaced   *the forest on weekends*

as animal and animal and animal from the car

ghosts tell or say — mouths gumming with paint

back when was one of the books we had to hide in the forest on weekends

made 'such a zoo' the table *medieval* a vast

spilled milk act drips the waiting dogs below

                                                                        snouts ascending

                              ...

a horrible woods

the guts of
some lily

                              ...

bright heft

muted & blues

papering

boats pulp –

if it's not water – rain.

resign

                    ...

refind

a vessel –

reform

as emptiness

following

                    ...

an historical note

behind them

vertical moats,

falls

      not a flute

           but violins

                 like crying

                        children a number

                              drains

        ...

the storm thickening

one lost in the red hull

or

one lost the red hull

or

one last red hull

or

one lost in red

or

one last red

or

haul one last lost

or

red hulls one lost

or

last *seen* as

last shorn

...

like hills, more

                  stutter

                        of crayon matter

sinking or floating

toys go here

                  ...

thin

bones

a stream

      so sun

        scoured

          belly

            -slick wreck I

              weathered

     ...

longing

swell

a sea

    in pencil

        candles carefully

            lapped

                    cliffs

                    climbing selves

                    etcetera

      ...

gums

the bells'

sway

                    (residue)

      ...

privilege

plays

   a part

making art

   of history,

      relationships

      other blurs

      that panoramic panic

...

   a graphite ledge

   hedge your fold

   human into a

   face form *our*

vulture as

the first

new word

learned here

...

stagger damp

      workmilk scrim

           skirt

             the morning

past children

carrying

liquid ships

        ...

                    small

                hands chalk

             the walls

        a boat

won't cave

will char

the sound

Plural
Bell

"No tongue tell"

in the flesh place

it was a tone

Vwail viol – wild

Thy shoult report

The wild dead body allowed

Well remember't

Orphan, sapfoot

Descending errata

Hysterical tissues (her)

Bulging historical

Jangling loose & bells

The raised lid stir
A pulpable sound

Wood the animal parts

An exhausted
Ladder her meat

"She *would*
  know"

The gal

Lows

                                    white tun

                                    -ic trans-

                                    fused w/

                                    threads of

                                    bark an *if*

                                    scapular

                                    sepulchre then

                                    churlish then

                                    scalpel from

which

her speech hung

behalve

behave

belong

Scrape side

Some rhyme

She was

As rupture inside

Another rupture

Etcetera bargain

The pain of its

For rapture

Gwhirl. Groanlimbs.

Like swims her solid

purts aroun' her must.

Tones efluent some

Thing in the vein of

It fits in limbs rose

Her thought

Herself

With others then

stupid or foolish

groundown

      her heights hung self-

boughed

      as fleeing as such

a sporrow

      bound to seen & loftily

'splayed

      rounded mass till time bent back in

to form

      shoved l'wer, stands, chants fences'

paleings

people

      still searching with chains

Languor over language

Broke take brook

Over

Concentrate her

Anywhere else on

Postpone the question

Over

Julia Drescher lives in Colorado where she co-edits the press *Further Other Book Works* with the poet C.J. Martin. Her work has appeared most recently in *'Pider, Entropy, Likestarlings, Aspasiology,* & *Hotel.*